BIRDS OF PREY

Written by Steve Parker
Illustrated by Treve Tamblin

HENDERSON
PUBLISHING PLC

© 1995 HENDERSON PUBLISHING PLC

BIRDS OF PREY - what are they?

They are birds who prey - meat-eaters, who hunt animals for their food. This book tells you about many different bird predators, large and small, from around the world. Their common feature is that they are all superb hunters.

Some prey on one main type of victim, such as mice, or other birds, or snakes. Others feed on almost anything, even the dead bodies of other animals, called carrion.

Raptors

Birds of prey that hunt mainly by day are called raptors. They include eagles, vultures, hawks and falcons. These are all members of the bird group *Falconiformes*.

A raptor's keen eyes can see victims thousands of metres away. Most can fly very fast, soar, dart, and hover in one place. They have sharp, curved beaks (bills) and talons (claws) to catch and rip up their prey.

Owls

Owls are not raptors. They are in a different bird group, *Strigiformes*. But they belong in a book about birds of prey, since they are also excellent hunters.

When raptors go to sleep, owls wake up. They hunt at night. They have huge eyes to see in the dark, and soft feathers for silent flight. Their hearing is amazing, and they too have sharp hook-like beaks and curved talons.

Big and small

The largest raptor is one of the largest birds in the world, the California Condor. Its wings are 3 metres across, and it weighs 11 kilograms. Sadly, it is also one of the rarest birds in the world.

The tiniest raptor is the pygmy falcon, whose head and body is only as big as your hand.

RAP-FAX

Each bird featured in this book has its own *RAP-FAX* panel. This tells you important Raptor Facts at a glance. It includes the scientific name, which is important because birds sometimes have different local names in different local languages.

Powerful wings

Large flight feathers on wings

Sharp, hooked beak (bill)

Keen eyesight

Smooth feathers on body

Tail fanned out for manoeuvring

Strong, curved talons (claws)

BIRDS OF PREY 3

NEW WORLD VULTURES

CALIFORNIA CONDOR

Scientific name	*Gymnogyps californianus*
How big?	140 centimetres head-to-tail, wingspan 300 centimetres
Where it lives	Californian mountains, USA
Favourite food	Carrion (dead animals)

A spectacular sight

The Californian condor is a spectacular bird, a great dark shape soaring on huge wings. It stays aloft for hours without flapping, using the breezes that blow through the mountains. As it soars, it peers at the canyons and lowlands with keen eyes, searching for signs of death far below.

New World Vultures

Condors are vultures from the continent of America (the New World). They look similar to the Old World vultures, but they are not close relatives.

Condors have hooked beaks to tear off strips of meat from the bodies of large animals killed by bears or wolves. They have long, featherless heads and necks, so they can poke right inside a body without clogging up with sticky blood. They cannot squawk or sing, only hiss and wheeze.

Mountain retreat

When the weather is no good for soaring, condors spend hours sitting quietly on a cliff, high in the mountains. They sunbathe, preen their feathers, digest their last meal and doze, until they are hungry again.

Pampered chick

During the spring breeding season, the male California condor flies a special display for his mate. The pair do not make a nest. The female lays one white egg in a mountain cave or on a ledge.
The parents incubate (keep warm) the egg for six weeks until the chick hatches. Then they feed and protect it for over a year! So they can only raise one chick every two years.

Near the end?

Condors are certainly splendid, though maybe not beautiful. In the past they were shot by hunters, and died after eating poisoned animals. Now there are only about a dozen left in the whole world. Conservationists are trying to breed more in San Diego Zoo. But it could be near the end for the huge California condor.

BIRDS OF PREY

SOUTH AMERICAN KING VULTURE

Scientific name *Sarcoramphus papa*
How big? 80 centimetres head-to-tail
Where it lives Forests and grasslands of South America
Favourite food Carrion, especially rotten fish

The fiercest king

When a king vulture lands at a carcass in the jungle, all the other birds leave! The fiercest of them all, in farming areas it even kills calves and sheep.

Most vultures find dead animals by sight. The king vulture is one of the few birds that has a good sense of smell. It sniffs out its food in the dense rainforests, where sharp eyes would not be much use.

Bright colours

The king vulture's bald head and neck are brightly coloured, but its body is mainly white, with black wings. It breeds in the spring, usually laying two white eggs in an old tree stump. The chicks hatch after about two months and stay with their parents for two years - a very long time in the bird world.

6 BIRDS OF PREY

TURKEY VULTURE

Scientific name	*Cathartes aura*
How big?	75 centimetres head-to-tail, wingspan 180 centimetres
Where it lives	Breeds in North America, migrates to South America to feed on open grassland in winter
Favourite food	Anything, especially rubbish

Waste not, want not
Vultures are nature's recyclers. They clean up dead bodies, so nothing is wasted. The turkey vulture is very good at this job. It eats almost any waste — meat and bones, rotten fruit or vegetables, even animal droppings. Farmers have killed turkey vultures for many years, because they thought the birds carried diseases to their animals. But this is not true.

Dull company
These dull brownish birds with red bald heads roost in trees at night, in groups of 30 or so. They take off in the day in great flocks, to search for food. In the spring they lay two splodgy brown eggs, in a cave or hollow log. Both parents care for the babies, which hatch six weeks later. The babies are fed on regurgitated food. This means it was eaten by the parent, partly digested, and sicked up again! Ugh!

BIRDS OF PREY

SECRETARY BIRD

Scientific name *Sagittarius serpentarius*
How big? 130 centimetres head-to-tail, 200 centimetres wingspan
Where it lives Grasslands of Africa
Favourite food Ground animals, especially snakes

Feet for walking

The secretary bird prefers to walk rather than fly. It strides slowly through the grassland, its long legs covering many kilometres each day. Its short, stubby toes are designed for walking, not grabbing and ripping as in other raptors.

Stamping and kicking

When the secretary bird spots something on the ground — a mouse, bird, insect or reptile — it runs towards it, and pecks it fiercely with its sharp beak. It even eats large snakes, which it kills by kicking and stamping on them, then flinging them into the air and smashing them onto the ground.

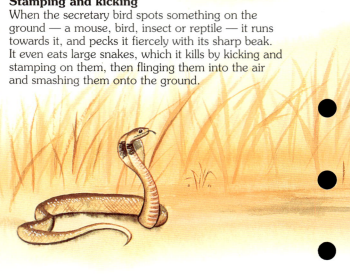

8 BIRDS OF PREY

Pen quills

This tall, black and white bird is named from the long feathers at the back of its neck. They look like the old-fashioned quill pens that secretaries and writers might have put behind their ears.

The rest of the secretary bird is a strange mixture. It has the long legs and tail of a stork, but the sharp, curved beak and powerful wings of an eagle. Scientists say it is a raptor, but it has a group all of its own.

High fliers

In early summer, the male secretary bird performs a wonderful flying display for his mate. They build a nest of sticks and grass high up in a tree. The female sits on the eggs for 45 days, while the male chases away other secretary birds. Both parents feed the chicks, on torn-up snakes and other scaly yummies.

BIRDS OF PREY

OSPREY

Scientific name *Pandion haliaetus*
How big? 60 centimetres head-to-tail
Where it lives Near water in North America, Europe and Asia in the summer, migrates south to coasts of Africa and Australia for winter
Favourite food Fish, small animals, carrion

Flying fisherman
The osprey is a superb fish-catcher. It flies high over the water, scanning the surface for fish, and hovering occasionally for a better look. Then it dives feet-first into the water, grabs a large fish with its claws (which are especially spiny for the purpose), and flaps back into the air.

Till death us do part

When an osprey finds a mate, at three or four years old, it's for life. Every spring, the male performs a breeding display for his long-time partner. He catches a fish, flies up into the sky, calls loudly, folds his wings, and drops like a stone back towards the ground.

Home from home

The osprey pair build a huge stick nest in the top of a waterside tree. They return every year and add more sticks to the nest. Finally it is too heavy and falls down. The birds have to start again.

The mother osprey lays between two and four brown speckled eggs, and sits on them for 35 days. For the following six weeks, the male brings fish for his partner to tear up and feed to the chicks.

World-wide raptors

Ospreys are found on every continent, though they only visit South America on winter migrations. For years, they were shot by hunters, and harmed by the poisons which farmers use to kill pests. These powerful birds disappeared from Britain in 1908. But they returned to Scotland in 1955, and now there is a small but thriving number of Scottish ospreys again.

BIRDS OF PREY

OLD WORLD VULTURES

AFRICAN WHITE-BACKED VULTURE

Scientific name   *Gyps africanus*
How big?   80 centimetres head-to-tail
Where it lives   Open plains of Africa
Favourite food   Carrion

A magic bird?
People used to think that vultures used magic to find their food. But they use their incredible eyesight, and watch their neighbours.

As the day hots up on the African plains, air currents begin to rise, and the vulture gets airborne. It cruises at great height, watching other vultures and ground scavengers like hyenas. If they move, the vulture follows. In this way, many vultures arrive as if by magic, at the fresh carcass of a zebra or wildebeest.

Queuing to eat
The vultures sometimes sit in a nearby tree, waiting for the lions and hyenas to finish eating. Then they hop to the body, and within a few minutes all that's left is the toughest bones.

Often the vultures stuff themselves with so much food that they are too heavy to fly. If danger threatens, they have to regurgitate some of it before flapping away.

12 BIRDS OF PREY

Old World vultures
Vultures that live in Europe, Africa and Asia are called Old World vultures. They are closer cousins of eagles and hawks than they are of New World vultures. But they look very similar to American vultures because they have a similar life style, feeding on carrion.

Not quite bald
Apart from its white back, this vulture is dull brown, with lighter brown underneath. Its head and neck are covered with fine brown down. It nests in the dry season, when plenty of animals die from drought and become food for the single chick.

BIRDS OF PREY

BEARDED VULTURE OR LAMMERGEIER

Scientific name *Gypaetus barbatus*
How big? 100 centimetres head-to-tail
Where it lives Mountains of Middle East and Africa
Favourite food Carrion, mainly bones

Fast flier
This sandy-coloured bird of prey, with black wings and a tiny black 'beard', lives high in the mountains. It glides faster than a car on the motorway, down over the plains to look for carrion. But usually it has to wait until larger vultures have eaten. So all it gets is the bones.

Broken bones
However, the bearded vulture has a smashing plan. It carries a bone into the air and drops it onto the rocks below, so it smashes open. The bird then lands and scoops out the bone marrow with its spoon-shaped tongue.

14 BIRDS OF PREY

EGYPTIAN VULTURE

Scientific name	*Neophron percnopterus*
How big?	70 centimetres head-to-tail
Where it lives	Open country of Africa and Middle East
Favourite food	Carrion, eggs, human waste

Any opportunity

The Egyptian vulture is an opportunist — it eats whatever and wherever it can. It is not afraid of people, raiding rubbish tips and following ploughs to pick up insects and worms. It even uses bits of rubbish to build its nest, and it eats bits of excrement from toilets!

Broken eggs

One of the smaller vultures, the Egyptian vulture waits near a carcass until the bigger birds and animals have eaten. Then it picks off the last tiny scraps of meat from the bones. It also steals flamingo eggs and chicks.

Stone hammer

This bird is one of the few animals to use tools. It can break open an ostrich or flamingo egg, by picking up a stone in its beak and throwing this at the egg. But it may have to try 20 or 30 times until it gets a shell-cracking direct hit.

BIRDS OF PREY

FALCONS

PEREGRINE FALCON

Scientific name *Falco peregrinus*
How big? 40 centimetres head-to-tail, wingspan 100 centimetres
Where it lives Worldwide, cliffs and mountains
Favourite food Other birds, mainly pigeons

Record breaker
No other bird matches the peregrine for both speed and accuracy in the air. This magnificent falcon can fly so fast, and swerve and swoop so quickly, that few of its bird victims escape.

Stoop to kill
The peregrine is famous for its steep dive, called a stoop. It flies high above its victim, such as a pigeon, folds its wings back, and power-dives at over 300 kph. The talons open and thud into the prey, in a flash of feathers and flesh, killing it at once. The peregrine then takes its meal to a special perch, to pluck and eat it.

The falconer's choice
Over 4,000 years ago in Asia, people started training birds of prey to help them hunt. From this developed the sport of falconry. It has been popular ever since, especially with rich rulers. In medieval Europe it was *the* sport of kings.

The best and most expensive falconry birds have always been peregrines, because of their spectacular flying feats. Gyr falcons, kestrels, merlins, goshawks and sparrowhawks can also be trained, as well as some owls.

16 BIRDS OF PREY

Poisoned chain

Peregrine falcons are in danger because they are harmed by the poisons used by farmers to kill insect pests. The poisoned insects are eaten by birds, who are then hunted by the peregrine. The great falcons become sick, they lay eggs with thin shells that break too soon, and they die in the cold winter. Around the world, conservationists work hard to save this spectacular raptor.

BIRDS OF PREY

GYR FALCON

Scientific name	*Falco rusticolus*
How big?	55 centimetres head-to-tail, wingspan 130 centimetres
Where it lives	Arctic tundra
Favourite food	Ptarmigan

Biggest falcon
This beautiful bird is the largest of all the falcons. It lives in the coldest places - the icy, treeless tundra of the far north, in the Arctic. It rarely comes south, even to breed.

Snowy falcon
Gyr falcons ("geer-falcons") can be any shade of white or grey. This helps them to stay unnoticed in the icy, snowy landscape. They hunt by flying close to the ground, and catch any small mammal or bird. The plump ptarmigan, king of partridge, is their favourite.

The female gyr falcon usually lays three or four browny eggs. But in years when food is plentiful, and there are lots of ptarmigan, she may lay six or seven. Many birds alter their egg numbers like this, according to the food supply.

18 BIRDS OF PREY

KESTREL

Scientific name	*Falco tinnunculus*
How big?	35 centimetres head-to-tail, wingspan 70 centimetres
Where it lives	Open places of Europe, Asia and Africa
Favourite food	Small mammals, reptiles and birds

Hover-bird

Most birds of prey can hover — stay in one spot in the sky, using tiny, rapid movements of their wings and tail. But the kestrel is the master-hoverer, and the one you often see along roadsides.

Silent and watchful

The kestrel finds small animals by hovering about 15 metres above the ground. It makes no noise, and watches for the slightest movements among the grass and leaves below.

Mice, voles, lizards and insects go about their business, unaware of the stationary shape above. But as soon as they move a leaf or scuttle across an open space, the kestrel falls silently out of the sky, to grab them in its sharp talons.

BIRDS OF PREY 19

HOBBY

Scientific name	*Falco subbuteo*
How big?	33 centimetres head-to-tail, wingspan 75 centimetres
Where it lives	Open places all over the world
Favourite food	Birds, insects, bats on the wing

Synchro-fliers

Hobbies are small falcons with long wings for expert flying. They catch almost all their prey in flight, often picking out one bird or insect from a large flock or swarm. The hobby can even outfly a swallow, swift or bat.

Most birds of prey perform a courtship flight, but a pair of hobbies are the champions of synchronized flying. They soar side by side high above their territory, then dive and dash and weave through the trees, exactly together. The male also does a solo flight, rolling over with his wings beating together to make a drumming noise.

Second-hand nests

Like many other raptors, hobbies use second-hand nests, like those of crows. They may add a twig or two, but flying is much more fun than nest-building!

BIRDS OF PREY

PYGMY FALCON

Scientific name	*Polihierax semitorquatus*
How big?	19 centimetres head-to-tail
Where it lives	African desert and scrub
Favourite food	Insects, small reptiles and birds

Tiny but noisy

The pygmy falcon is the smallest raptor, a tiny white killer with blue-grey wings and back. It is unusually noisy, too. When it is alarmed, it makes a high-pitched call that rises up the musical scale.

The pygmy falcon rarely soars and glides. It perches on a high twig, flicks its tail and bobs its head, and waits for insects to buzz past. Then it flies out and grabs them.

Breed when you can

Like many desert animals, this mini-falcon has no regular breeding season. It raises a family whenever the rains come, and there are enough insects and small animals to feed to its chicks. The nest is an empty one of another bird, even the delicate dangling globe of a weaver bird.

BIRDS OF PREY

HAWKS AND EAGLES

RED KITE

Scientific name *Milvus milvus*
How big? 60 centimetres head-to-tail, wingspan 150 centimetres
Where it lives European meadows and woodlands
Favourite food Any small animal

The hawk group

Kites belong to the group of raptors called *Accipiters,* which includes hawks, eagles and buzzards. Many hawks have specialized diets, but kites do not. They feed on almost anything they can get. Their long wings have rounded tips, and the tail is deeply forked.

Common to rare

Red kites eat worms and insects, frogs and lizards, mice and voles, small birds and even carrion. Four hundred years ago, they were one of the commonest birds around London. Now they have almost disappeared from Britain, except for parts of Wales.

Kites in Europe fly south to Africa for the winter. When they migrate, they form large flocks that hunt together and roost in trees at night.

22 BIRDS OF PREY

Soft nest

Red kites sometimes make their own nests in the treetops. But like other raptors, they prefer to use a ready-made nest, especially of a heron. The pile of twigs is a metre across, and the kite parents line it with soft things, from moss and grass to rags and paper.

The female sits on her two to four white speckled eggs for about a month. Then she and her partner feed the chicks for another six weeks.

Kite cousins

The red kite has a smaller cousin called the black kite. It lives in European forests near ponds, lakes and rivers. The black kite feeds on scraps of fish left by herons and cormorants, and on frogs and other small bank side animals. This bird has also adapted well to humans, and feeds happily on rubbish tips.

EVERGLADE KITE

Scientific name   *Rostrhamus sociabilis*
How big?   38 centimetres head-to-tail
Where it lives   Florida Everglades, USA
Favourite food   Snails!

Seizing snails

The Everglade kite is quite unlike other kites, because it only eats one kind of food. Snails. Its beak is longer and narrower than in other raptors, because it is specially designed for winkling snails out of their shells.

The kite flaps slowly over the pools and creeks of the swampy Everglades. When it spies a snail, it swoops down and grabs the hard-shelled meal with one foot, and takes it back to a perch to eat.

Stabbing snails

The kite stands on one foot, holds the snail shell in the other foot, and waits. Eventually the snail starts to come out of its shell. Quick as a flash, the kite stabs with its beak and kills the prey. Then it shakes the shell off and swallows the hapless mollusc.

24   BIRDS OF PREY

BAT HAWK

Scientific name *Machieramphus alcinus*
How big? 45 centimetres head-to-tail
Where it lives Tropical rainforests of Asia and Africa
Favourite food Bats

Bats or nothing
Like snail kites, bat hawks are fussy feeders. Their name tells you their food. No other raptor specializes in bats, and no other raptor hunts so late in the day. As dusk falls, the bat hawk waits near a cave or hollow tree, where bats have slept through the day.

Dinner at dusk
As the sun sets, the bats stream out in flocks. The bat hawk darts among them and grabs one with its talons. It then moves the victim to its beak and carries it like this back to its perch. Other raptors carry prey in their claws.

If the bat hawk wants a second helping, it must feed quickly. The evening rush hour is soon over and the bats fly off into the night.

BIRDS OF PREY 25

HONEY BUZZARD

Scientific name	*Pernis apivorus*
How big?	60 centimetres head-to-tail, wingspan 120 centimetres
Where it lives	Woodlands of Europe and Asia
Favourite food	Honey

Food fad

The honey buzzard, as you might guess, is another bird of prey with a food fad. It loves honey! It tears open the nests of bees and wasps with its strong claws, licks up the honey and snaps up the grubs. Its special stiff feathers help to stop it being stung. And it even eats the adult bees, delicately nipping off the stings at the rear end before swallowing them.

Be my honey, honey-b
Like many raptors, male and female honey buzzards have their own area, called a territory. They chase away others of their kind. Honey buzzards also defend the bee and wasp nests in their territory.

The male flies along and claps his wings over his head, to impress his mate. The female usually lays two eggs, in a large treetop stick nest lined with leaves.

Single parent
These birds are careful parents. They take turns to feed and guard the young, and clean out and repair the nest. As they swap duties, they clap beaks together and call "kee-er" loudly.

If one of the parents is lost or dies, the other carries on and raises the chicks alone.

South for the winter
After the breeding season, some honey buzzards from northern areas fly south, to spend the winter in warm Africa. If they cannot find bees' nests there, they eat termites, ants and other small creatures.

HEN HARRIER

Scientific name	*Circus cyaneus*
How big?	50 centimetres head-to-tail, wingspan 100 centimetres
Where it lives	Open country of Europe and North America
Favourite food	Small animals

Low-speed manoeuvres

Falcons are the champion high-speed birds of prey, but harriers are best at low-speed aerobatics. These accipiters have long wings and tails, to give good lift even when flying slowly. They glide low, scanning the ground for movements and listening for rustles.

The hen harrier has a round, owl-like face, which helps its keen ears to pick up the tiniest sounds.

V-winged hunter

The hen harrier hunts for mice and other small rodents, reptiles, frogs, insects and injured birds. It flies low and to and fro in a regular pattern, quartering the area, with its wings held in a V-shape above its back.

This hunting technique works best in open country with low vegetation. So the hen harrier likes grassland, fields, heaths and moors, and especially swamps. In America it is often called the marsh hawk.

When the harrier spots something, it drops down to the ground and stabs the prey with its talons.

Nest on the ground

Most birds of prey nest high in trees or mountains. The hen harrier nests on the ground, in the undergrowth. The pair court in flight, then build a mound of twigs and leaves, often near other nesting hen harriers.

Mid-air food swop

The female sits on her five white eggs for a month, and the brighter-coloured male does the hunting. When he returns, he does not land. The female flies up, turns upside-down, and grabs the food from his talons.

BIRDS OF PREY 29

AMERICAN BALD EAGLE

Scientific name	*Haliaeetus leucocephalus*
How big?	100 centimetres head-to-tail, wingspan 220 centimetres
Where it lives	Lakes, rivers and coasts of North America
Favourite food	Fish

Lucky escape

This great eagle is one of the most famous animals in the world. It is the national bird of the USA. Yet not long ago, it was almost wiped out. Bald eagles were shot by fishermen, who thought they ate too many fish. And they were poisoned by pesticide chemicals, which washed from fields into rivers, and got into their fish prey.

Today, bald eagles are protected by law. They have been bred in zoos, and released into the wild. Hopefully they seem to be out of danger.

Not bald, just white

The 'bald' eagle is not bald, but it looks so, because of its white head and neck feathers. These birds have an amazing courtship flight. The male and female rise into the sky together, lock talons, and tumble back down, swooping away before they crash to the ground.

30   BIRDS OF PREY

Giant nest

Bald eagle parents build a huge nest on a treetop or cliff ledge. They add more twigs and leaves each year. The nest may grow to three metres across and three metres deep - a record size for a bird's nest!

Fish on most days

The ugly bald eagle babies stay in the nest for 10 weeks, squabbling over food. Often the youngest is killed in the arguments.

Bald eagles eat fish of all kinds, fresh or dying or dead. At the end of the nesting season, some of them fly to Alaska. Here they find an easy catch - exhausted salmon, struggling up river to breed.

AFRICAN FISH EAGLE

Scientific name	*Haliaeetus vocifer*
How big?	80 centimetres head-to-tail
Where it lives	Rivers, lakes and swamps of Africa
Favourite food	Water life, mainly fish

Anything that swims

The African fish eagle lives near water, and it hunts anything that swims - fish, birds and frogs, dead or alive.

Early in the morning, several fish eagles sit on tree branches above a lake or river, looking for prey. They attack almost any kind of fish and water bird, even flamingoes. But they do not enter the water, like ospreys. The fish eagle swoops just above the water's surface and grabs the prey in its talons.

Noisy colonies

Compared to most birds of prey, fish eagles are very noisy. They make loud yelps and squawks as they dance and display to each other in the evening. They also build the usual eagle-type nest, a pile of sticks and twigs called an eyrie, in a tree or cliff, or on the ground.

BIRDS OF PREY

HARPY EAGLE

Scientific name	*Harpia harpyja*
How big?	100 centimetres head-to-tail, wingspan 240 centimetres
Where it lives	Rainforests of South America
Favourite food	Monkeys and other animals

The biggest eagle
The harpy is the world's largest eagle. It flies gracefully through the forest, slowing down near big trees to listen for animal noises. When it hears a chattering monkey, a snoring sloth or a snuffling opossum, the harpy swerves through the branches. It pierces the victim with talons bigger and stronger than your fingers.

In grave danger
Harpies lay their eggs in the usual stick-built eagle eyrie (nest), at the very top of the forest canopy. They probably breed every two years. These huge, powerful birds are protected by law. But the rainforests where they live are disappearing fast, and their feathers and feet are prized targets for poachers. Sadly, the number of harpies is falling fast.

BIRDS OF PREY

GOLDEN EAGLE

Scientific name	*Aquila chrysaetos*
How big?	80 centimetres head-to-tail, wingspan 190 centimetres
Where it lives	Mountains of Europe, Asia and North America
Favourite food	Rabbits and hares

Eagle boots

The golden eagle belongs to the group of true eagles, which have 'boots' on their legs. The feathers grow right down to the ankles. Other raptors have bare, scaly legs.

The golden is one of the most common and widespread eagles. Its feathers are brown rather than gold, except for its golden head and neck.

Lazy killer

The golden eagle never hurries. It perches on a high branch or rocky crag for hours, surveying the scene. Then it flaps slowly into the sky and soars leisurely, peering across the countryside for rabbits, hares and other prey. If it sees a victim, the golden eagle dives swiftly, stabs with its talons, and carries the limp body back to its eating perch.

False tales

Golden eagles take ground birds such as grouse, and they also feed on carrion. Farmers and shepherds dislike them, because they see the eagles carrying away young sheep and goats. However, these animals may have been sick or dead already. The eagle is just cleaning up carrion.

Lots of nests

The male and female soar and tumble for each other before mating. They often have several nests, which are huge baskets of sticks high on cliff faces. They use the nests in turn, tidying up one each year.

The pair raise two chicks. One hatches before the other - and in many cases, it pecks its younger sister or brother to death. This may sound horrible. But it ensures that if food is short, at least one chick will have the chance of survival.

WEDGE-TAILED EAGLE

Scientific name	*Aquila audax*
How big?	80 centimetres head-to-tail, wingspan 250 centimetres
Where it lives	Outback of Australia
Favourite food	Rabbits, hares, similar animals

Wedge shape
This massive, glossy, dark brown bird is Australia's largest bird of prey, and the fourth largest in the world. Also called the eagle hawk, it is fairly easy to identify as it soars high overhead, by its great size and wedge-shaped tail.

A tickly perch
Between hunting flights, this eagle perches on a tree - or a large ant-hill! The ants may crawl among its feathers and get rid of fleas and other pests. Then the eagle sails high above the outback, looking for prey such as rabbits, hares and small wallabies.

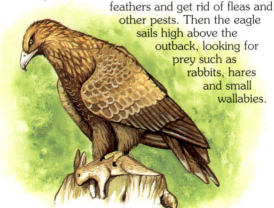

Protected birds
In the dry Aussie scrublands, animals are always dying. The carcass of a kangaroo or sheep attracts several eagles, who feed like vultures. Wedge-tails were shot by sheep farmers, for killing their lambs. Now they are protected by law.

Life partnership

Like many big birds of prey, these eagles pair for life. The breeding season starts in July, but if there is a drought, they do not bother. The birds swoop and dive and call "pee-ya, pee-ya" and "yes-sir, yes-sir" to each other. They smarten up their usual stick eyrie in a tall gum tree, and line it with fresh leaves.

The female sits on two purple-and-brown eggs while the male brings her food. The new babies look ugly and straggly, like all eagle chicks, but by 10 weeks old they are ready to fly.

BIRDS OF PREY 37

NORTHERN GOSHAWK

Scientific name	*Accipiter gentilis*
How big?	50 centimetres head-to-tail, wingspan 120 centimetres
Where it lives	Forests and lowlands of Europe, Asia and North America
Favourite food	Medium-sized birds

Bird-killer

Goshawks are strong and aggressive killers, often used for falconry. They can swerve and dash through the branches of forest trees, and catch birds almost as big as themselves. Pheasants, grouse, owls and even herons are killed, pierced and crushed by the goshawk's huge talons. The victim is then plucked and eaten on the ground.

A noisy duet

The goshawk meets its usual partner each year, and they repair the same nest at the top of a pine tree. They perform flying displays, and every morning they scream a harsh-sounding song together.

The number of eggs depends on if it's a good year (when it can be five) or a bad one. He hunts for food and she shares it among the babies, to prevent squabbles. You know what young children are like!

38 BIRDS OF PREY

SPARROWHAWK

Scientific name	*Accipiter nisus*
How big?	35 centimetres head-to-tail, wingspan 70 centimetres
Where it lives	Woodlands of Europe and North Africa
Favourite food	Small birds

No escape
The sparrowhawk specializes in chasing small birds like, er, sparrows. It zig-zags through the trees at high speed, and the prey can only escape by diving into a thick bush. The sparrowhawk brings its quarry to a special branch and plucks out the feathers with its beak, before tearing up the flesh.

Hawk pellets and killer chicks
The nest is at the top of a spruce tree, and lined with hair. The next-door tree is used for roosting. Here the sparrowhawk 'coughs up' or regurgitates lumps called pellets. These contain hard bits that it cannot digest, like beaks and legs. Bringing up pellets is unusual for hawks, but common among owls.

Sparrowhawks start their killing early. The oldest chick usually eats the others as they hatch!

BIRDS OF PREY 39

BUZZARD

Scientific name	*Buteo buteo*
How big?	55 centimetres head-to-tail, wingspan 120 centimetres
Where it lives	Woodland of Europe, Asia, Africa
Favourite food	Mice, rabbits, small animals

Sit and wait
Buzzards are the most common large raptors in Europe. They may circle in rising air, or hover near the ground, but they are not busy fliers. The buzzard prefers to sit, and wait, and wait, and wait.

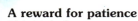

A reward for patience
This bird of prey may sit still for hours, until a mouse, rabbit, lizard, or even insect, wanders past below. Then it drops onto the victim and kills it on the ground. Buzzards may hang about near mouse holes and rabbit warrens for most of the day, until the occupants venture out.

40   BIRDS OF PREY

Excited once a year

Despite this boring killing method, buzzards get quite excited at breeding time, in spring. The male and female flap and soar and circle high in the sky, dive down and swoop back up again, and make a "kee-iw" mewing noise as they greet each other.

The buzzard's twig nest is high on a tree or cliff, and lined with soft leaves, moss, hair and even seaweed. The male brings food for the female and babies.

A tough start in life

As the young birds grow up, they must leave the nest — and the area. Many birds of prey 'own' their patch of land, or territory. They chase away others, and this includes their own grown-up offspring. So the new adults must roam far and wide in their first year, looking for a free territory. But most territories are taken, and the owners defend them fiercely. If a buzzard cannot find a vacant area, it may not survive.

BIRDS OF PREY 41

CRESTED SERPENT EAGLE

Scientific name   *Spilornis cheela*
How big?   60 centimetres head-to-tail
Where it lives   Forests of Asia
Favourite food   Snakes

Spots and stripes
In most birds of prey, members of the same kind (species) look much the same, wherever they come from in the world. Crested serpent eagles do not. They vary in size and the colour of their feathers, and in the height of the head crest.

Scaly, sliding prey
These birds often soar high in the air, calling to each other, but they are not hunting. They are courting and marking out their territory.

The serpent eagle does not chase prey. It sits on a forest branch, and waits patiently for tree snakes to slide past. It grabs the snake with its talons, which have specially roughened toes to grip the slithery meal. Then it tears off long strips of flesh and swallows them like spaghetti.

42 BIRDS OF PREY

AFRICAN HARRIER HAWK

Scientific name	*Polyboroides typus*
How big?	60 centimetres head-to-tail
Where it lives	Forests of southern Africa
Favourite food	Baby birds (boo! hiss!)

Yellow skin
This hawk does not look like a baby-killer. It has long legs and a long black tail, a smart grey body, a striped black-and-white front, and bright yellow skin around its eyes and beak. It feeds on small forest creatures and the fruits of the oil palm tree. But what it really likes to eat is baby birds...

Tree climber
Most raptors are specialized for flying. But the African harrier hawk is not. It's a climber. It clambers through tree branches, looking for birds' nests. It even hangs upside down from a twig and pokes its sharp claws into tree holes, or into the fragile nests of weaver birds. If it grabs a chick or egg, that's the end of that.

BIRDS OF PREY 43

OWLS

BARN OWL

Scientific name *Tyto alba*
How big? 35 centimetres head-to-tail, wingspan 80 centimetres
Where it lives Worldwide, open country, woods, towns
Favourite food Rodents and other small animals

Killers in the dark

Owls are night-time birds of prey. Like raptors, they have sharp, curved beaks and talons. Their huge eyes, taking up over half the head, can see amazingly well in the dark. And their hearing is incredibly good. If you had the eyes and ears of an owl, you would never be afraid of the dark, because you could see and hear everything.

A bad omen

The eerie shriek of the barn owl was thought to signal evil. Now we know they are only calling to their mate, or to neighbours in the next territory.

Barn owls live all over the world. They are soft-golden above and white below. They inhabit barns, of course, and also roofs, lofts, church steeples and warehouses, as well as the cliff crevices and tree holes that were their original homes.

Farmer's friend

Barn owls eat mice, voles, small rats and many other rodents, who are pests because they eat farm crops. The owl flies silently, looking and listening. It cannot swivel its eyes, so it moves its whole head to peer around and pick up the slightest rustles. Then it swoops talons-first and impales the unfortunate rodent, or perhaps a small bird.

Owl pellets

Most owls swallow their prey whole, but they cannot digest it. So they 'cough up' or regurgitate the hard parts, like the bones, teeth, feet and skin. This comes out as a rounded pellet, about as big as a thumb. The ground beneath the owl's favourite eating perch is littered with these pellets.

BIRDS OF PREY 45

TAWNY OWL

Scientific name	*Strix aluco*
How big?	35 centimetres head-to-tail, wingspan 90 centimetres
Where it lives	Woods and gardens of Europe, Africa and Asia
Favourite food	Small rodents and birds

Too-whit-too-whoo

The tawny owl is the most common owl in Europe, and is the one that makes the famous "too-whit-too-whoo" hooting call. It lives in woods, parks and wooded gardens, and does not migrate.

During the day, the tawny owl dozes in a tree fork. But you would not notice it, because its plumage is mottled brown to blend in perfectly with the tree bark.

Death on silent wings

At night, the tawny owl sits on a hunting perch and peers into the darkness, watching and listening for small mammals, lizards and other reptiles, frogs and other amphibians, and large insects.

When it detects a prey, the owl flaps gently towards it. Owl feathers have soft, slightly furry edges, for silent flight. The victim notices nothing until the talons stab into its back.

46 BIRDS OF PREY

SNOWY OWL

Scientific name	*Nyctea scandiaca*
How big?	60 centimetres head-to-tail, wingspan 150 centimetres
Where it lives	Arctic tundra
Favourite food	Lemmings

Snowy disguise

The white plumage of this beautiful bird gives a clue to its habitat. It lives in the treeless lands of the far north, called the Arctic tundra, which are covered by snow for many months each year. The white feathers help the owl to blend in with its background, which is called camouflage.

Daytime hunter

The snowy is unusual among owls, since it hunts by day. It flies low over the ground, slowly fluttering near to its prey. It kills a wide variety of prey, such as Arctic hares, stoats, ptarmigan, ducks and gulls. But its main food is the vole-like creature called the lemming.

Snowy owl chicks in the nest eat two lemmings each day, and in a good year, there may be more than 10 chicks for the parents to feed.

BIRDS OF PREY 47

GREAT HORNED OWL

Scientific name *Bubo virginianus*
How big? 60 centimetres head-to-tail, wingspan 150 centimetres
Where it lives North and South America
Favourite food Small mammals

Biggest and best
The great horned owl is the biggest and strongest owl in America. Like many owls, it has 'horns' or ear tufts. But these are just long feathers, and have nothing to do with hearing. The owl's ears are lower down on the sides of its head.

The hunter hunted
These owls live in open country and woods, and also in city parks and gardens. They keep the same territory throughout the year, chasing away rivals and intruders.

Great horned owls use third-hand nests. They take over the nest of a raptor, which was already second-hand. And they are very powerful predators. They hunt ground squirrels, rabbits, mice and any other small animals. They even turn the tables on the usual cat versus bird battle, by killing and eating pet cats.

48 BIRDS OF PREY